PRAYERS
TO
MARY

PRAYERS TO MARY

**The Most Beautiful Marian Prayers
Taken from the Liturgies of the Church
and Christians throughout the Centuries**

Compiled and Edited

by

MOST REV. VIRGILIO NOE

*Secretary of the Sacred Congregation
For Divine Worship*

Illustrated

CATHOLIC BOOK PUBLISHING CORP.
New Jersey

NIHIL OBSTAT: Daniel V. Flynn, J.C.D.
Censor Librorum

IMPRIMATUR: ✠ Joseph T. O'Keefe, D.D.
Vicar General, Archdiocese of New York

This book was originally published in Italian by
Edizioni Messaggero, Padova, Italy, under the title,
Preghiere a Maria. The English translation is by
Anthony M. Buono.

Icons of the Virgin Mary (except p. 35) © Monastery
Icons—www.monasteryicons.com. "Mother of
Tenderness (p. 35) © Sister Regina Krushen, OSB,
Abbey of St. Walburga.

(T-210)

© 2007, 1987 by Catholic Book Publishing Corp., N.J.
Printed in the U.S.A.
ISBN 978-0-89942-210-7
www.catholicbookpublishing.com
3 4 5 6 7 8 9 10 11 12 13 14 15

PREFACE

ONE way of linking together all the days of May (or any period that we wish to devote to Mary) is to take up and make our own some of the prayers that Christians throughout the ages have used to invoke our Lady and to express their love for her.

In this way, the continuous commemoration of Mary over the course of a designated period has a new reason every day for exalting our Lady's beauty and her sublime privileges. The daily encounter with Mary becomes an occasion to reinforce the motivating idea upon which the soul lives that day and to experience the presence of Mary more intimately and deeply, more cheerfully and carefully. Thus, the time spent with Mary is translated into a source of consolation for us.

"Your thoughts, O Mary, are full of tenderness, and your custom is to love human beings." Such is the foundation for our trust, according to the Ethiopic Liturgy.

The prayers found herein are taken from relatively few sources—some less known Liturgies and the minds and hearts of saints and sinners, poets and simple folk. (An Appendix also gives some of the more well-known traditional prayers to Mary.)

However, they are prayers that reflect all situations. And this is enough to root in us the conviction that "the prayers to the Blessed Virgin are prayers of reserve for times when we do not succeed in praying any other way. There is not even one such prayer that the most wretched sinner cannot say in all truth. Indeed, in the plan of salvation, prayer to Mary is the ultimate recourse: with it we can never be lost" (Charles Péguy).

The prayers are so different in tone that it should be easy for us to find one that corresponds to our own tone or mood and adapt ourselves to the sentiments it sets forth.

The assistance of a prayer that preserves and develops the sense of the mystery of Mary can elicit in us the basic attitudes of admiration, trust, and love toward our Lady.

Of course, the mystery of Mary cannot always be expressed in a loud voice. Sometimes, we must assume another attitude: "It is difficult to exalt you, O Virgin, with hymns that express our love, as we would like to do. It is easy for us to love you in silence, without any fear" (Byzantine Liturgy).

Just as it is true that before God "silence is praise of Him," so is it at times even in the case of Mary and her mystery. We must find it spontaneous and easy to love our Lady in contemplative silence.

Virgilio Noé

CONTENTS

WE FLY TO YOUR PATRONAGE

This is the most ancient prayer to Mary. A succession of invocations indicates an acute awareness of the straits in which humankind struggles along.

A series of encomiums exalts Mary the Mother of God, ever Virgin, who is glorious and blessed. It also expresses a most profound understanding of the heart of Mary and of her place in the work of Redemption.

WE fly to your patronage,
O holy Mother of God;
despise not our petitions
in our necessities,
but deliver us always from all dangers,
O glorious and blessed Virgin.

3rd CENTURY

YOU SURPASS ALL PRAISE

This prayer, found in Egypt, was chiseled by an anonymous hand on a terra-cotta. It derives from the 3rd or 4th century. The text is inspired by the angel's salutation to Mary.

O immaculate Virgin,
  Mother of God,
full of grace,
the One Whom you brought forth, Emmanuel,
is the fruit of your womb.

In your Motherhood
you have nurtured all human beings.
You surpass all praise and all glory.

I salute you,
Mother of God,
joy of the Angels,
because you surpass in fullness
what the Prophets have said about you.

The Lord is with you:
you gave life to the Savior of the world.

3rd-4th CENTURY

TURN YOUR EYES TOWARD ME

St. Ephrem the Syrian is one of Mary's greatest cantors. He has exalted her in her privileges and in her unique perfection: "You, O Christ, and Your Mother are the only ones who are beautiful under every aspect, because there is no uncleanness in You, O Lord, and no stain in Your Mother."

St. Ephrem also speaks in a notable fashion about the action that Mary exercises over the lives of Christians. He guides the faithful to invoke Mary as Mother and Mediatrix and to take refuge in her with humble and filial trust: "Mary is the hope of those exiled who can attain reconciliation and reenter paradise."

Owing to the elegance of his writing style, St. Ephrem has been called the "lyre of the Holy Spirit." In addition, his Mariological teaching has earned him the title of "Marian Doctor."

MOST Holy Lady, Mother of God,
   you are the only one completely pure
in soul and body,
and you surpass all purity,
all virginity, and all chastity.

You are the sole dwelling place
of all the grace of the Spirit,
and you far surpass the Angels in purity
and in holiness of soul and body.

Turn your eyes toward me.
I am sinful and impure
and stained in soul as well as in body
with the passions and pleasures
that constitute the weeds of my life.

Set my spirit free from its passions.
Sanctify and restrain my thoughts
when they race toward adventurism.
Regulate and divert my senses.
Shake off the detestable and infamous
   tyranny
of my impure inclinations and passions.
Destroy in me the empire of sin.

Grant wisdom and counsel to my spirit
that is filled with darkness and wretchedness.
Help me to correct my faults and my failings.
Then, set free from the night of sin,
may I be worthy to glorify and exalt you
without reserve,
O sole true Mother of the true Light,
Christ our God.

Alone with Him and through Him,
you are blessed and glorified
by every visible and invisible creature,
now and forever.

ST. EPHREM THE SYRIAN

MOTHER OF LIFE

"Love and veneration for the Virgin Mary constitute the soul of Eastern piety, its heart, that which warms and animates the whole body" (Bulgakov, *Orthodoxy*).

This love of the East for Mary is apparent in the names with which Mary is invoked: the All-Holy, the Virgin of Compassion, the Virgin who heeds us quickly, the Virgin who saves from sorrows, the Virgin of the sweet kisses, the Virgin who nurses, and the Virgin who indicates the way.

However, there is a constant and authentic harmony in the Eastern prayer to the Blessed Virgin: Mary is never separated from the mystery of Christ. This trait is exemplified in the icons where the all-pure Mother always has her Son next to her.

HOW can we fail, O all-holy one,
to admire your Divine and human child-
    bearing!
O all-immaculate one,
without the help of a man,
you brought into the world
a Son Who has no father according to the
    flesh.

He is the Word begotten in eternity by the
    Father,
without mother.

He suffered no change, admixture, or division
but integrally retained the characteristics of
    each nature.

O Lady and Virgin Mother,
beseech Him to save the souls of those who,
in true faith,
acknowledge you as the Mother of God.

The Prophet David
who, for your sake, was an ancestor of the
    God-Man,
addressed the following words, in his hymns,
to the One Who has done great things in you:
"The Queen takes her place
at Your right hand" (Psalm 45:10).

God has chosen you to be
the productive Mother of life.
He became a human being in you,
without a human father,
in order to restore in human beings
the image of Himself that had been tarnished
    by sin.
He did so to lead back to His Father
the little sheep lost on the mountains,
carrying it on His shoulders,
to reunite humankind with the Powers of
    heaven,
and so save the world,
O Mother of Christ the Lord
Who is rich in mercy!

BYZANTINE LITURGY

STAR ILLUMINED BY THE SUN

In the Byzantine Liturgy, prayers to Mary are frequently woven out of images taken from the pages of Scripture. The Biblical tone is a dominant note of this piety. We could say there is no Scriptural text that directly applies to the Virgin (or can be applied to her in an accommodated sense) that has not been used, commented on, or paraphrased in the Byzantine Liturgy.

In the following passage, the titles applied to Mary are so numerous as to constitute a true litany of glory for the Mother of God.

Mary appears as the end point for many moments of the History of Salvation that are recounted in the Bible from Genesis to the Books of Kings. The Blessed Virgin is compared to the heavenly stairway that God made use of to come to earth and renew it.

From that time, the sun of Christ illumines the world, and Mary shines on that world as a star guiding human beings from death to life.

HAIL, star illumined by the sun, hail:
through you creation has been renewed.

You are the heavenly stairway
through which God has descended.

You are the earth
of the fruit that never perishes.

You are the key
to the doors of paradise.

You are the burning bush
that is not consumed.

You are the sea
that drowns the spiritual Pharaoh.

You are the rock
that gives forth water for the thirsty.

You are the column of fire
that guides those who are in darkness.

You are the nutriment
that has replaced the manna.

You are the promised land
flowing with milk and honey.

You are the tabernacle
of God and the Word.

You are the Ark
gilded by the Holy Spirit.

You are the censer of gold and perfume
giving forth the holy fragrance of Christ.

BYZANTINE LITURGY

WE GLORIFY YOU

The faithful, whether at home or in church, feel the Blessed Virgin's gaze on them. Mary looks out on them from domestic icons or from the central apses of the sanctuary.

The most frequent greeting addressed by the faithful to Mary in the liturgical Office or in prayers recited at home is the one given below. By its frequency it occupies the same place in the East that the Hail Mary has in the Marian devotion of the West.

YOU are more venerable than the Cherubim and incomparably more glorious than the Seraphim.

Without losing your virginity,
you gave birth to the Word of God
and are truly the Mother of God.
We glorify you.

BYZANTINE LITURGY

YOU ARE THE BULWARK OF VIRGINS

In every age prayers in honor of Mary have flourished. Every generation has expressed its love for Mary by means of invocations known as the most beautiful and imaginative, the most rich in theology, and the most fruitful for true devotion. One such prayer is the Akathist Hymn, the most celebrated and most popular of the hymns of the Eastern Liturgy in honor of Mary.

This hymn was composed for the feast of the Annunciation on the occasion of a miraculous deliverance of Byzantium attributed to the Blessed Virgin. It manifests a people's firm gratitude to Mary.

Today the Akathist Office is assigned to Saturday of the fifth week of Lent, and it constitutes a true Marian feast.

O Virgin, Mother of God,
you are the bulwark of virgins
and of all who have recourse to you.
The Creator of heaven and earth
has made you Immaculate
so that He might dwell in your womb
and might teach all to exclaim:

Hail (*or* Rejoice), pillar of virginity.
Hail (*or* Rejoice), gate of salvation.

Hail (*or* Rejoice), initiator of spiritual fullness.

Hail (*or* Rejoice), dispenser of the Divine goodness.

Hail (*or* Rejoice), because you have regenerated
  those who were conceived in sin.

Hail (*or* Rejoice), because you have restored wisdom
  to those who were deprived of reason.

Hail (*or* Rejoice), you who have crushed the corruptor of minds.

Hail (*or* Rejoice), you who have given birth to the source of chastity.

Hail (*or* Rejoice), nuptial bed of pure marriages.

Hail (*or* Rejoice), you who reconcile the faithful
  to the Lord.

Hail (*or* Rejoice), beautiful nourisher of virgins.

Hail (*or* Rejoice), you who dress the holy souls as spouses.

Hail (*or* Rejoice), O immaculate Bride.

AKATHIST HYMN

MOTHER OF THE LAMB

In this strophe of the Akathist Hymn, Mary is greeted as the Mother of Christ, the Lamb Who will be immolated and the Shepherd Who guides and defends the flock. The hymn also celebrates Mary's protection and defense of us until we enter the sheepfold of heaven, because she is the gate of heaven.

HAIL (*or* Rejoice), Mother of the Lamb and the Shepherd.

Hail (*or* Rejoice), sheepfold of the spiritual flocks.

Hail (*or* Rejoice), shelter against invisible enemies.

Hail (*or* Rejoice), entrance to the gates of paradise.

Hail (*or* Rejoice), because heaven embraces earth.

Hail (*or* Rejoice), because earth sings together with heaven.

Hail (*or* Rejoice), perennial voice of the Apostles.

Hail (*or* Rejoice), unshakable courage of the Martyrs.

Hail (*or* Rejoice), solid bulwark of the faith.

Hail (*or* Rejoice), radiant sign of grace.

Hail (*or* Rejoice), you through whom hell was rendered armorless.

Hail (*or* Rejoice), you through whom we were reinvested with glory.

Hail (*or* Rejoice), O immaculate Bride.

AKATHIST HYMN

BLESSED ARE YOU, O MARY

Syria has always enjoyed a rich lyrical tradition dedicated to singing the praises of Mary. The Church of Antioch rendered a special cult to the Mother of God even before the Council of Ephesus: the events that have marked the Nestorian crisis bear witness to the great extent to which belief in Mary's Divine Motherhood was diffused among the faithful and rooted in their hearts.

Prayer texts are rich in a theology centered on the Divine Motherhood. Their poetry is simple and characterized by a penetrating tenderness.

Among the great Marian hymnists besides Ephrem the Syrian is numbered James of Sarug (451-521). The Syrian-Maronite Liturgy borrows heavily from his lyrical treasures.

BLESSED are you, O Mary,
and blessed is your holy soul,
for your beatitude
surpasses that of all the Blessed.

Blessed are you who have borne, embraced,
and caressed as a baby
the One Who upholds the ages
with His secret word.

Blessed are you, from whom the Savior
appeared on this exile earth,
subjugating the seducer
and bringing peace to the world.

Blessed are you, whose pure mouth touched
the lips of the One Whom the Seraphim
do not dare to look upon in His splendor.

Blessed are you, who have nourished
with your pure milk
the source from Whom the living obtain life
    and light.

Blessed are you, because the whole universe
resounds with your memory,
and the Angels and human beings celebrate
    your feast. . . .

Daughter of the poor,
she became the Mother of the King of kings.
She gave to the poor world
the riches that can make it live.

She is the bark laden with the goodness
and the treasures of the Father,
Who sent His riches once again
into our empty home. . . .

JAMES OF SARUG

CONSUMED BY SORROW

Romanos the Melodist (6th century) ranks first among the great chanters who gave to the Byzantine world the most beautiful liturgical hymns. Out of his deep religious spirit, Romanos draws forth a sincere poetic inspiration that is frequently manifested in an intimately dramatic form.

One example is the hymn *Mary at the Foot of the Cross,* which is paralleled by the *Stabat Mater* ("At the Cross Her Station Keeping") in the West. Mary is presented as a sheep who follows the Lamb as He is led to the slaughter, so that she may act as the sorrowful witness to the sacrifice.

L IKE a sheep
   that contemplates its lamb led to the
     slaughter,
Mary followed Him.

She was consumed by sorrow
with the other women,
and she said:
"Where are You going,
my Son?

"Why are You finishing Your course so
    quickly?
Is there another wedding at Cana,
where You must hasten to change water into
    wine?

"Can I go with You,
my Son,
or must I wait for You?

"Say something to me,
O Word,
and do not pass me by in silence:
You Who kept me pure,
You Who are my Son and my God."

ROMANOS THE MELODIST

WE ARE POOR

Germanus of Constantinople (8th century) is an important witness to the Marian devotion of the East, and his name is almost on a par with the names of St. John Damascene and St. Andrew of Crete. The sermons of Germanus abound in admirable prayers to the Blessed Virgin, all prompted by filial confidence.

When Germanus speaks of Mary, or when he has recourse to her, his accents seem to anticipate those of St. Bernard.

WE are poor in Divine gifts,
O Mary,
but through you
we see the riches of kindness offered to us.
Therefore, we say with confidence:
the earth is full of the mercies of the Lord.

Rejected by God
because of the multitude of our sins,
through you we seek Him out again,
rediscover Him,
and are saved.

Therefore, O Mother of God,
grant us your powerful help
so that we may attain salvation.
And obtain for us the aid of your Son,
the sole Mediator necessary with God.

For your magnificence is infinite,
your goodness in helping the needy is inexhaustible,
and the number of your benefits is limitless.

No one achieves salvation except through you,
O most Immaculate One!
No one receives grace except through you,
O most Chaste One!
And no one obtains mercy except through you,
O most Honored One!

Who would then fail to call you blessed?

I will call you—
who were enriched by your Son and God—
glorious and blessed,
and I will praise you with all generations.

ST. GERMANUS OF CONSTANTINOPLE

ADMINISTRATOR OF TREASURES

Mary holds a large place in the Chaldean Liturgy, especially in the daily liturgy of the Divine Office. The Mother of Jesus is present there in the abundance of Biblical images and in the invocations with which the faithful entrust the world, the Church, and sinners to her protection.

Together with exquisite and perfect praises, the prayers affirm once again the universal intercession of Mary.

For the feast of the Immaculate Conception, the prayer to Mary blends inspired poetry with the precise doctrine of the Immaculate Conception: through the merits of Christ's Blood, Mary was set free from original sin. The Son accomplished redemption in the Mother in a way highly superior to that of all other descendants of Adam. He did not leave her in the power of the evil one—not even for an instant.

Mary's exceptional position does not cut her off from the children of the Church. On their behalf she is the administrator of the treasures that God has placed in her hands and in her heart.

QUEEN of queens, rich in all things,
  enrich your servants with benefits,
O Mother of the Most High!
He has made you administrator of His treas-
    ures
and Universal Lady,

just as it has pleased the King of kings
to set you above all things.
In your goodness,
pour down upon all persons the gifts they
    need,
so that the whole world may forever weave
a crown of thanksgiving to you.

How beautiful you are,
O Virgin Bride,
for the glorious Bridegroom
[Who is] the Divine Word!
He placed His treasures in your womb,
and in you as in a great ocean
He brought together all graces
and made you the source of life for all mor-
    tals. . . .

You are merciful in all necessities!
Come to the aid
of all the children of the Church
now and at the hour of their death.

CHALDEAN LITURGY

WE SALUTE YOU, O MARY

St. Cyril of Alexandria was the champion of Mary's Divine Motherhood against the opposition of Nestorius. At Ephesus, after the Council (444) had upheld the Divine Motherhood, Cyril preached a famous homily. He addressed the Virgin Mary with words that expressed the sentiments of all Christian souls and the traditional Faith, already set forth in the first of twelve anathemas:

"If anyone does not profess that Emmanuel is truly God and in consequence the Blessed Virgin is the Mother of God (*Theotokos*) because she has brought forth in flesh the Word of God made flesh, let him be anathema."

WE salute you, O Mary,
    Mother of God,
treasure of the universe,
inextinguishable flame,
crown of virginity,
scepter of the true Faith,
indestructible temple,
tabernacle of the One Whom the world cannot
    contain,
and Mother and Virgin. . . .

In your virginal womb
you enclosed the Immense and Incomprehensible One.

Through you
the Trinity is glorified
and the Cross is celebrated and adored
everywhere on earth.

Through you
the heavens exult with joy,
the Angels and Archangels are glad,
demons are put to flight,
the demon temptor is cast out of heaven,
and our fallen nature has again been assumed
into heaven. . . .

It is through you
that the only-begotten Son of God,
Who is the Light,
shone amid the nations
who were seated in darkness and the shadow
of death.

What human voice can ever worthily celebrate
the ineffable greatness of Mary?
She is Mother and Virgin
at the same time.
Through her
peace has been restored to the world.

What peace?
Our Lord Jesus Christ,
Whom Mary has brought forth!

ST. CYRIL OF ALEXANDRIA

PRAY TO HIM AS HIS MOTHER

In the hymns of the ferial office of the Chaldean Liturgy, one of the strophes is always in honor of Mary. It combines theological depth of thought with poetic sensitivity.

THE Church said to Mary:
  "Come, and we will go together
to pray to the Son of God
for the sins of the world.

"You will pray to Him
because you have nursed Him,
and I will pray to Him
because I have mingled His Blood with my
    nuptials.

"You will pray to Him as His Mother,
and I will pray to Him as His Bride.
He will listen to His Mother
and respond to His Bride."

CHALDEAN LITURGY

HOLY VIRGIN, I BEG YOU

St. Ildephonsus of Toledo, Spain, was proclaiming the joy of being "a servant of Mary" already in the 7th century. In one of his prayers he brings to full light the idea of Mary's virginal Motherhood as a model of spiritual life for the Christian.

Mary must obtain for us from the Holy Spirit the grace for Christ to be formed spiritually in us just as she, through the power of the same Spirit, fashioned Christ according to the flesh.

HOLY Virgin, I beg you:
enable me to receive Jesus from the Spirit,
according to the same process
by which you bore Jesus.

May my soul possess Jesus
thanks to the Spirit
through Whom you conceived Jesus.

May the grace to know Jesus
be granted to me through the Spirit
Who enabled you to know how to possess Jesus
and bring Him forth.

May my littleness show forth
the greatness of Jesus
in virtue of the Spirit
in Whom you recognized yourself
as the handmaid of the Lord,
desiring that it be done to you
according to the word of the Angel.

May I love Jesus
in the Spirit
in Whom you adored Him as your Lord
and looked after Him as your Son.

ST. ILDEPHONSUS OF TOLEDO

O ALL-HOLY SERVANT AND MOTHER

In the Liturgy of the Visigothic Church the prayers are woven essentially from Biblical texts, solidly grounded in theology, and enriched with true emotion.

Prayers abounding in their formulation span the centuries and echo the notes of blessing and invocation of Mary that resounded in ancient Spain.

Possibly for the first time in the history of Marian devotion, these prayers speak of Mary's spiritual Motherhood, and they highlight the maternal ways of the mercy of God that are present in her.

They also inculcate the devotion of the "slavery" of love of Mary and the attitude of filial confidence to have toward Mary.

Because of these features, such prayers have an air of relevance about them.

O All-holy Servant and Mother
of the Divine Word,
childbirth revealed you to be a virgin
and virginity made you fruitful.

Gather in your devout embrace
the people who have recourse to you.

In your profound mercy
take care of the flock
that was redeemed by the Blood of the Son
Whom you have brought forth.

Show yourself a Mother to creatures,
for you gave nourishment to their Creator.
Bless with your service those whom you see
offering themselves to you in homage.

Grant that we may be protected by your inter-
     cession
for we exult in bearing
the sweet yoke of your servitude.

And grant that all of us who have sung praises
     in honor of your conception
may continue to live in your service,
so that once the stain of sin has been removed
we may attain the One
Whose Mother we honor you to be
by our celebrations.

Defend us now and forever
with your inexhaustible affection
so that the One Whom you brought forth
may possess us eternally in His Kingdom.

VISIGOTHIC BOOK OF PRAYER

GIVE CHRIST TO US

Ambrose Autperto lived in the Abbey of St. Vincent at Volturno during the 8th century. In a sermon for the purification of Mary, Ambrose speaks of our Lady's spiritual Motherhood, and he grounds it on our fraternity of grace with Christ. If Mary loves us from the heights of heaven, it is because she sees in us the children that she brought forth when she gave birth to her Son Jesus.

When Mary offered Christ to Simeon, she offered Him to all of us as well, and through her intercession she continues to offer Him—both to the elect, whom grace already unites with Christ, and to sinners, who are separated from Christ.

In Mary, according to Ambrose Autperto, there are found a mystical Motherhood and a Motherhood of intercession.

I beg you, Blessed Virgin,
give Christ to us through your intercession,
for you cannot say no to your children.

Indeed, you even overlook the injuries
committed against you
by those children who do not honor you as they
should.

For all who are overcome with love for their
　children
put up even with irreverence.

Therefore, protect with your fervent prayers
those who are unworthy of your benefits
yet have been brought forth by you
in your only-begotten Son.

Pray to Him
for the transgressions that many of them com-
　mit.

AMBROSE AUTPERTO

REJOICE AND BE GLAD

This enthusiastic Marian text from the Ambrosian Liturgy provides us with an ancient canticle in praise of Mary's virginal Motherhood.

This praise of Mary is completed by the praise of the Savior, of Whom Mary is the Mother. The source of the text is probably Eastern.

The religious sentiments that delight our Marian devotion today are therefore the very ones that moved the Christian people of the East and the West in the face of Mary's beauty.

REJOICE and be glad,
for you are the exultation of the Angels.

Rejoice, O Virgin Divine,
for you are the jubilation of the Prophets.

Rejoice, O blessed one,
for the Lord is with you.

Rejoice, for at the announcement of the Angel
you accepted into your womb the One
Who gives happiness to the world.

Rejoice, for you gave birth to the Creator
and absolute Ruler of all things.

Rejoice, for you were found worthy
to become the Mother of Christ.

AMBROSIAN LITURGY

GOD IS OUR BROTHER

In St. Anselm of Canterbury (d. 1109) the Benedictine tradition of trust in Mary "Mother of Mercy" receives its precise doctrinal form. Overwhelmed by spiritual sluggishness and the fear of sin, the soul can always take refuge in Mary.

St. Anselm underlines the will of God to be merciful toward a sinful world, giving to it His Son with a kind of "new creation" in which Mary has the role of Mother: the Mother of Christ, Judge and Redeemer, and the Mother of human beings who have become brothers and sisters of Christ.

"The One Who was able to create all things out of nothing did not will to recreate, without Mary, what had been stained. God is therefore the Father of created things, and Mary is the Mother of 'recreated' things. God is the Father Who constituted all things, and Mary is the Mother who reconstituted all things."

Such are the words of St. Anselm. He then goes on to ask—with complete confidence—for the grace to share in Christ's filial devotion toward His Mother and in Mary's love for her Son.

O Blessed Lady,
   you are the Mother of Justification
and those who are justified;
the Mother of Reconciliation
and those who are reconciled;

the Mother of Salvation
and those who are saved.

What a blessed trust, and what a secure refuge!
The Mother of God is our Mother.
The Mother of the One in Whom alone we
hope
and Whom alone we fear
is our Mother! . . .

The One Who partook of our nature
and by restoring us to life
made us children of His Mother
invites us by this to proclaim
that we are His brothers and sisters.

Therefore, our Judge is also our Brother.
The Savior of the world is our Brother.
Our God has become—through Mary—our
Brother!

ST. ANSELM OF CANTERBURY

BY THE GRACE YOU FOUND

For St. Bernard, Mary constituted the object of his personal meditations as well as his instructions to the monks at Citeaux. In writing or speaking about our Lady he was simply following the inclination of his own heart. The Saint lived the recommendation he made to others: We must fix our eyes on the Blessed Virgin not only with a quick glance but with a prolonged and loving gaze, which leads to invocation and contemplation.

To insure that our trust in Mary will be truly filial, St. Bernard presents our Lady as our advocate with Jesus, just as Jesus is our advocate with the Father. Since Mary is the way by which the Lord came down to us, she must also serve as the ladder by which we climb up to Him.

O blessed Lady, you found grace,
brought forth the Life,
and became the Mother of salvation.
May you obtain the grace for us to go to the
Son.
By your mediation,
may we be received by the One
Who through you gave Himself to us.

May your integrity compensate with Him
for the fault of our corruption;

and may your humility, which is pleasing to
    God,
implore pardon for our vanity.

May your great charity cover the multitude
of our sins;
and may your glorious fecundity confer on us
a fecundity of merits.

Dear Lady,
our Mediatrix and Advocate,
reconcile us to your Son,
recommend us to Him,
and present us to your Son.

By the grace you found,
by the privilege you merited,
by the Mercy you brought forth,
obtain for us the following favor,
O blessed Lady.

May the One Who—thanks to you—came
    down
to share our infirmity and wretchedness
make us share—
again thanks to you—
His glory and beatitude:
Jesus Christ, your Son, our Lord,
Who reigns in heaven and is blessed forever!

ST. BERNARD

WE LOVE YOUR MERCY

The loving devotion that St. Bernard had toward Mary did not allow him to speak about her without directly addressing the Blessed Virgin with the sentiments that poured out of his heart. Because of the trust he had in Mary, he did not hesitate to bind her in this way.

O blessed Virgin,
did anyone ever invoke you in need
and yet fail to receive help?
Only such a person could remain silent
about your mercy.

As for us, who are your poor servants,
we congratulate ourselves for you
on account of all your other virtues,
but we rejoice in your mercy
in a special way for ourselves.

We praise your virginity,
and we admire your humility;
but your mercy has an even sweeter taste
for us sinners.
We have a preferential love for your mercy,
we remember it more often,
and we invoke it more frequently. . . .

Who then could measure,
O blessed Lady,
the length and breadth, height and depth
of your mercy?

Its length extends indeed until the last day,
so that you may come to the aid
of all who invoke it.
Its breadth spans the whole world,
so that the whole earth is full of your mercy.

Its height is such that it brought about
the restoration of the heavenly city.
Its depth achieved the redemption of those
who sat in darkness and the shadow of death.

Thanks to you,
heaven has been populated,
hell has been emptied,
the ruins of the heavenly Jerusalem have been
    rebuilt,
and the unfortunate people living in hope
have been given back the life they had lost!

Thus it is that your charity,
so powerful and at the same time so gentle,
pours forth in abundance,
manifesting itself tenderly
and lending assistance effectively.

ST. BERNARD

DAUGHTER OF YOUR SON

St. Bernard has been called the *harp of Mary,* because when he speaks about the glories of our Lady his words constitute a true music. The Marian devotion of the Abbot of Clairvaux was so proverbial during the Middle Ages that Dante in the *Divine Comedy* chose him as his guide in paradise toward the throne of Mary.

Once he has reached the throne, Bernard intones a hymn in honor of the Blessed Virgin that resounds with the echo of the sermons he preached on earth.

O Virgin Mother, daughter of your Son,
humble and exalted beyond every creature,
and established term of God's eternal plan,

you are the one who ennobled human nature
to such an extent that its Divine Maker
did not disdain to become its workman-
ship. . . .

O Lady, you are so great and powerful
that those who seek grace without recourse to
you
are expecting wishes to fly without wings.

Your loving kindness not only comes to the
     aid
of those who ask for it but very often
spontaneously precedes the request for it.

In you is mercy, in you is pity,
in you is magnificence, in you is found
everything that is good in God's creation.

DANTE (Paradise, XXXIII)

O MARY, BLESSED ARE YOU

Among the prayerful meditations of St. Catherine of Siena, the following in honor of Mary is one of the most admirable—for its doctrine, for its filial tenderness toward the Mother of God, and for its poetic language embellished by new and sensitive expressions.

Catherine prayed in these words on March 25, 1379. It was the day of her 32nd birthday, and she was at Rome.

O Mary, Mary, temple of the Trinity.
O Mary, bearer of fire.
O Mary, dispenser of mercy.
O Mary, restorer of human generation,
because the world was repurchased
by means of the sustenance
that your flesh found in the Word.
Christ repurchased the world with His Passion,
and you with your suffering of mind and body.

O Mary, peaceful ocean.
O Mary, giver of peace.
O Mary, fruitful land.
You, O Mary, are that new plant
from which we have the fragrant flower

of the Word, Only-begotten Son of God,
because this Word was sown in you,
O fruitful land.
You are the land and the plant.

O Mary, vehicle of fire,
you bore the fire hidden and veiled
beneath the ash of your humanity.

O Mary, vase of humility,
in which there burns the light of true knowl-
edge
with which you lifted yourself above yourself
and yet were pleasing to the eternal Father;
hence He took and brought you to Himself,
loving you with a singular love.

With this light and fire of your charity
and with the oil of your humility,
you drew and inclined His Divinity to come
into you—
although He was first drawn to come to us
by the most ardent fire of His inestimable
charity.

Today, O Mary, you have become a book
in which our rule is written.
In you, today, is written the wisdom
of the eternal Father.
In you, today, is manifested
the strength and freedom of human beings.

I say that
the dignity of human beings is manifested
because when I look at you, O Mary,
I see that the hand of the Holy Spirit
has written the Trinity in you,
forming in you the incarnate Word,
the Only-begotten Son of God.

He has written for us the wisdom of the Father,
that is, the Word.
He has written for us His power,
because He was powerful
in effecting this great mystery.
And He has written for us
the clemency of that Holy Spirit,
because only through grace and the Divine
    clemency
was so great a mystery ordained and accom-
    plished.

But today I ardently make my request,
because it is the day of graces,
and I know that nothing is refused
to you, O Mary.
Today, O Mary, your land has generated
the Savior for us.

O Mary,
blessed are you among women throughout the
    ages!

ST. CATHERINE OF SIENA

YOU HAVE GIVEN US THE FLOWER
OF THE SWEET JESUS

The brilliant mind of Catherine of Siena immerses itself in the essential mysteries of the Faith: the Incarnation and the Redemption. In them Catherine discerns the presence of Mary.

In the Incarnation, Mary is the *blessed and sweet field* in which the Word has been sown. In the Redemption, because of her perfect adherence to the will of her Son, Mary is disposed to *make of herself a ladder* for placing Jesus on the Cross.

O God,
how inestimable and most sweet is Your Love,
and how sweet is the union You have effected with human beings!
You have splendidly shown Your ineffable Love
through many graces and benefits heaped on creatures,
and especially through the benefit of the Incarnation
of Your Son;
that is, the grace of seeing the Highest One
come down to the lowest—which is our humanity.

Rightly should human pride be abashed
on seeing God so abased
in the womb of the Virgin Mary,
who was that sweet field in which was sown
the seed of the Word Incarnate,
the Son of God.

Truly, most dear Father,
in this blessed and sweet field of Mary
God grafted this Word in her flesh,
like the seed that is cast on the ground,
which by virtue of the sun's heat germinates
and brings forth flowers and fruits,
while the pod remains in the earth.

This is what God truly did,
by virtue of the heat and the fire
of the Divine Love
that He had for the human race,
casting the seed of His Word
in the field of Mary.

O blessed and dear Mary,
you have given us the flower of the sweet
Jesus.

And when did this sweet flower produce its
fruit?
When there was grafted in her
the wood of the most holy Cross:
because then we received perfect life.

And why did we say
that the pod remains in the earth?
What was this pod?
It was the will of the Only-begotten Son of
    God,
Who, as Man, was imbued with the desire
to honor His Father
and to bring about our salvation.

So strong was this immeasurable desire
that He hastened like someone enraptured—
sustaining pain and shame and vituperation—
to the opprobrious death of the Cross.

Consider, then, venerable Father,
that this same desire was in Mary,
that is, that she could not desire anything
    other
than the honor of God and salvation of crea-
    tures.
Moreover, the Doctors declare—
in manifestation of Mary's immeasurable
    charity—
that she was willing to become a ladder her-
    self
so as to place her Son on the Cross
if there had been no other way to do so.

And all this came about
because the will of the Son had remained
in her.

ST. CATHERINE OF SIENA

O MARY, APPEASE YOUR SON

This brief composition of Thomas à Kempis (d. 1471) presents the words and sentiments of a devout soul weeping over the sufferings of Mary. It is almost as if we were before a statue of the Pietà: we contemplate it and are moved.

O Mary, purple rose, white jewel,
  you who are tender, good, and full of love,
appease your Son.

That Babe you brought forth
filled with joy at the Angels' song,
you now receive from the Cross
into your sorrowful arms.

Have compassion on Christ and His Mother,
O faithful soul,
if you want to exult with them eternally in
    heaven.

Jesus, Son of God, have pity on me,
in virtue of the prayers of Your holy Mother.

Save me by means of the Cross,
lead me to the true light, I pray,
together with You in heaven.
You Who promised paradise to the good thief,
forgive me;
I am guilty,
but You redeemed me with Your Blood.

THOMAS á KEMPIS

O JESUS LIVING IN MARY

It has always been the conviction of the Christian people that the life of Christ can be better penetrated with the aid of Mary and through the imitation of Mary.

Our Lady is the most perfect image of Christ. It is the Mother who fashions us according to the model of Christ and who transforms the whole Church.

We can see this point in the magnificently rich prayer composed by Father John J. Olier (d. 1657). In it Christian piety is developed with a sure hand, culminating in union with Christ through Mary.

O Jesus living in Mary,
come to live in Your servants,
with Your spirit of holiness,
in the fullness of Your power,
in the perfection of Your ways,
in the truth of Your virtues,
and in the communion of Your Divine Mysteries.

In Your Spirit
and for the glory of the Father,
overcome every hostile power!

JOHN J. OLIER

AS A LITTLE CHILD I LOVED YOU

The Marian anthology of Pope Leo XIII is surprisingly rich and varied, not only with encyclicals about the Blessed Virgin but also with Latin poems written in honor of Mary.

In his poetry, the aged Pontiff tells Mary of his love for her, which grows with the years, and asks for her protection in life and in death.

AS a little child,
I loved you like a Mother.
Now that I am old,
my love for you has grown.

Receive me in heaven
as one of the blessed,
and I will proclaim
that I have obtained
such a great prize
through your patronage.

LEO XIII

IT IS SWEET MUSIC

IT is sweet music to the ear to say:
I salute you, O Mother!
It is a sweet song to repeat:
I salute you, O holy Mother!

You are my delight, dear hope, and chaste
    love,
my strength in all adversities.

If my spirit
that is troubled
and stricken by passions
suffers from the painful burden
of sadness and weeping;
if you see your child overwhelmed by misfor-
    tune,
O gracious Virgin Mary,
let me find rest in your motherly embrace.

But alas,
already the last day is quickly approaching.
Banish the demon to the infernal depths,
and stay close, dear Mother,
to your aged and erring child.

With a gentle touch,
cover the weary pupils
and kindly consign to God
the soul that is returning to Him.

LEO XIII

PLEASE BE MINDFUL,
O QUEEN OF THE PROMISE

Chartres and the Virgin of the Cathedral constituted the turning point for Charles Péguy on the pathway of his return to God.

The Blessed Virgin is the goal of his pilgrimage: when his son becomes ill, Péguy sets out to entrust him to our Lady. Mary keeps track of his steps and rewards his faith.

WHEN people will have placed us
in a narrow tomb,
when they will have celebrated over us
absolution and the Mass,
please be mindful,
O Queen of the Promise,
of the long pilgrimage we made. . . .

O Refuge of Sinners,
we ask for nothing more
than the last place in your purgatory—
so that we may weep at length
for our tragic history
and contemplate from afar
your youthful splendor.

CHARLES PÉGUY

I COME, O MOTHER,
TO GAZE ON YOU

The first spiritual relationship with the Blessed Virgin is simply a glance: *I come solely to gaze on you.*

What sustains that glance is not an articulated prayer but the song of the heart, which is given voice by love for Mary.

Praise precedes petition—indeed the latter cannot do without the former.

Is this not the case when people truly love one another?

IT is noon.
 I see the church open,
and I must enter.

Mother of Jesus Christ,
I do not come to pray.
I have nothing to offer
and nothing to request.

I come solely to gaze on you,
O Mother.
To gaze on you,
weep for joy,
and know this:
that I am your child and you are there.

I come only for a moment
while everything is at a standstill,
at noon!

Just to be with you,
O Mary,
in this place where you are.
Not to say anything
but to gaze at your countenance,
and let the heart sing
in its own language;
not to say anything
but solely to sing
because my heart is overflowing.

For you are beautiful,
because you are immaculate,
the woman fully restored in Grace,
the creature in its first honor
and its final bloom,
as it issued from God
on the morn of its original splendor.

You are ineffably intact,
because you are the Mother of Jesus Christ,
Who is the Truth in your arms,
and the only hope and the sole fruit.

PAUL CLAUDEL

MARY, THE MOTHER OF JESUS

Some modern prayers, constructed on a Biblical background and in discreetly poetic language, exalt Mary as the sacrament of the tenderness of God and as the Mother of love.

L ORD Jesus,
all generations proclaim
your Mother blessed.
In You she has found happiness.
Have mercy on us if we seek happiness
anywhere else.

Lord Jesus,
You exalted Your Mother:
You raise up the humble.
Have mercy on us if we humiliate the humble.

Lord Jesus,
You worked wonders for Mary.
What would she not have done for You?
Have mercy on us if we do not know
how to remain in awe before her.

PIERRE TALEC

WE ARE LOST

This prayer is the invocation to the Virgin of Girkalnis, a little city in Lithuania. It was written by a Lithuanian young woman deported into Siberia during the persecution of Stalin.

The prayer represents one bead in the Rosary of Marian devotion that in the course of the centuries has made Lithuania *the land of Mary.*

WE are lost,
we are tired and frozen. . . .
But you have not abandoned us,
O Mother of Mercy,
in the days of sorrow and misfortune.

O Mother,
to whom shall we have recourse,
upon whom shall we call,
in this hour of great misfortune?

Cast your glance, O Mother,
upon our hearts racked
with anguish and nostalgia;
see our lips discolored
by cold and hunger.

Make us return to the land
that Heaven itself has given us,
the land of crosses and churches,
the land that you have loved for centuries.
Enable us to see once more
the images that are famous for their graces,
your sanctuaries.

Grant us
to be able to sing together once again
hymns of gratitude and love
to the Merciful Jesus and to you,
O Mother of Mercy,
who have promised to obtain
the pardon of all faults. Amen.

LITHUANIAN YOUNG WOMAN

BE PRESENT IN OUR MIDST

MARY,
you were born without sin:
be present in our midst.

We need to know
that in our midst
someone has never wasted any talent.

That someone is you:
the only Woman!

PIERRE TALEC

FOUNT OF LOVE

L ORD Jesus,
in a unique manner
You are perfectly a Son.

You have crowned Your Mother
"with love and tenderness."

We give You thanks
for allowing this fount of love
to pour out upon all Your Church.

PIERRE TALEC

YOU ARE OUR MOTHER

O Mary,
look upon the Church,
look upon the most responsible members
of the Mystical Body of Christ
gathered about you to thank you
and to celebrate you as their Mystical Mother.

O Mary,
bless the great assembly of the hierarchical
  Church,
which also gives birth to brothers and sisters
  of Christ,
the firstborn among redeemed humankind.

O Mary,
grant that this Church of Christ—
in defining itself—
will acknowledge you
as its most chosen Mother, Daughter, and
  Sister
as well as its incomparable model,
its glory, its joy, and its hope.

We ask you now
that we may be made worthy of honoring you
because of who you are
and because of what you do
in the wondrous and loving plan of salvation.
Grant that we may praise you,
O holy Virgin!

O Mary,
look upon us who are your children,
look upon us who are brothers and sisters,
disciples and apostles and continuations,
of Jesus.
Make us aware of our vocation and our mission;
may we not be unworthy to take on—
in our priesthood, in our word,
in the offering of our life
for the faithful entrusted to us—
the representation and personification of Christ.
O you who are full of grace,
grant that the priesthood that honors you
may itself also be holy and immaculate.

O Mary,
we pray to you
for our Christian brothers and sisters
who are still separated
from our Catholic family.
See how a glorious group of them
celebrate your cult with fidelity and love.

See also how among another group,
who are so intent on calling themselves Christians,
there now dawns the remembrance and the veneration of you,
O most holy Lady.

Call these children of yours
to the one unity
under your motherly and heavenly aid.

O Mary,
look upon all humankind,
this modern world in which
the Divine Will calls us to live and work.
It is a world that has turned its back
on the light of Christ;
then it fears and bemoans the frightening
    shadows
that its actions have created on all sides.

May your most human voice,
O most beautiful of virgins,
O most worthy of mothers,
O blessed among women,
invite the world to turn its eyes
toward the life that is the light of human
    beings,
toward you who are the precursor-lamp of
    Christ,
Who is the sole and the highest Light of the
    world.

Implore for the world
the true understanding of its own existence;
implore for the world
the joy of living as the creation of God
and hence the desire and the capacity

to converse—by prayer—with its Maker,
Whose mysterious and blessed image
it reflects within itself.

Implore for the world
the grace to esteem everything as the gift of
    God
and hence the virtue to work with generosity
and to make use of such gifts wisely and prov-
    idently.

Implore peace for the world.
Fashion brothers and sisters
out of persons who are so divided.
Guide us to a more ordered and peaceful so-
    ciety.

For those who are suffering—
today there are so many and ever new ones,
afflicted by current misfortunes—
obtain solace;
and for the dead, obtain eternal rest.

Show yourself a Mother to us:
this is our prayer,
O clement, O loving, O sweet Virgin Mary!
Amen.

PAUL VI

QUEEN OF THE UNIVERSE

O Virgin Mary,
Mother of the Church,
we entrust to you
the entire Church. . . .

You are the "Help of Bishops";
protect and assist bishops in their apostolic
   work
as well as all priests, religious, and laity
who aid them in their difficult task.

At the moment of His redeeming death,
your Divine Son gave you as Mother
to the beloved disciple;
be mindful now of the Christian people
who entrust themselves to you.

Be mindful of all your children;
join to their prayers
your special power and authority with God;
keep their faith whole and lasting;
strengthen their hope;
and increase their love.

Be mindful of those who find themselves
in hardship, in need, and in danger,
and especially those who are persecuted
and kept in chains because of their Faith.
Ask for strength of soul for them,
O Virgin Mother,

and hasten the longed-for day
of their rightful liberation.

Turn your eyes of mercy
toward our separated brothers and sisters,
and be pleased to unite them to us,
for you brought forth Christ,
the meeting point between God and people.

O temple of spotless and never-fading light,
intercede with your only-begotten Son—
Mediator of our reconciliation with the Father
   (cf Rom 5:11)—
so that He may pardon our failings,
eliminate all discord from our midst,
and grant us the joy of loving one another.

We commend the entire human race
to your Immaculate Heart, O Mary.
Lead it to acknowledge Christ Jesus,
the one true Savior.
Keep from it all calamities provoked by sin.
Bring it peace in truth, justice, liberty, and love.

Grant that the whole Church, . . .
may raise up to the majestic God of mercy
the hymn of praise and thanksgiving,
the hymn of joy and exultation,
for the Lord has done great things
through your intercession,
O clement, O loving, O sweet Virgin Mary.

PAUL VI

HEAR, O MARY

O Mary most holy,
in your immaculate conception,
you are the creature of predilection,
the Daughter of God the Father Almighty,
raised to the summit
of His plan of mercy for all humankind.

You are the humble and admirable Mother
of our Lord Jesus Christ,
and thereby Mother of God,
that is, of the Word Incarnate,
Son of God and Son of Man,
our Savior.

You are the most pure Bride of Ineffable Love,
the Holy Spirit,
mysterious principle of the Incarnation
that took place in your inviolate womb.

O Mary,
accept our act of renewed and unanimous devotion,
with which we intend to acknowledge and celebrate
the election that God has made of you,
who are unique and blessed among all women,
assigning you a sublime and providential place
in the redemptive plan for humankind.

In this way,
O most pure Virgin,
God caused to shine forth
the transcendent idea of innocent human
   beauty,
elevating you into an exemplary mirror
of ready obedience to the Divine Will;
an incomparable and accessible example
of faith, hope, and love;
and a model for us
of silent and joyful contemplation
of the Divine plans
as well as of solicitous and gentle communion
with the vicissitudes of human suffering.

Hear, O Mary,
our filial voice,
interpreter of the heart of the whole Church, . . .
as we implore your special heavenly assistance
in this critical hour
for the spiritual and secular destiny
of the world.

To you,
O spiritual Mother
of the Mystical Body of Christ,
which is the Church,
we entrust our conscious Christian commit-
   ments,
assumed at our holy Baptism,

and we confirm them in the spirit of re-
newal, . . .
which must be a sign of our witness
as living members of the Catholic Church.

To you,
O Mother of the Church,
we therefore entrust our resolve of reconciliation:
reconciliation with God;
reconciliation with our brother and sister
human beings;
longed-for and perfect reconciliation with all
believers
in our Master and Redeemer, your Son Jesus
Christ;
an ever-promoted reconciliation in justice and
liberty,
and in the cooperation of the different social
categories;
reconciliation, finally, among peoples and nations
in the vigilant and sincere spirit
of security, collaboration, and peace.

To you,
O Mary,
source of Life,
we entrust the hopes of young people,
in their concerned search
for a more just and more human world,

and we confidently ask
that you direct their steps toward Christ,
the firstborn of renewed humankind,
so that in His light
their efforts can be joined
and their hopes come true.

Queen of Mercy,
O Mary,
hear the sighs of the suffering,
the cry of the oppressed,
the pleas of those who hunger and thirst for
    justice,
and obtain for them
that suffering may be assuaged,
that the right thing may be recognized,
and that the desire for true liberty may be
    realized.

Holy Guardian of the Eternal Word,
O Mary,
hasten the time of the total union
of those who acknowledge Christ
as the one Savior and Mediator.

Servant of God and Daughter of Zion,
turn your eyes toward your people
who have issued from the faith of Abraham.

Ark of the new Covenant,
intercede for all those who,

although redeemed by Christ,
do not yet know the light of the Gospel.

Mother of the Risen Lord,
and Mother of those reborn in Christ,
O Mary,
grant to us your children
the spirit of the beatitudes,
the love that believes all things
and hopes all things,
and the wisdom of the Cross,
so that after death has been overcome
we may reach the radiant dawn
in which the Christian hope
will be transformed into eternal possession.
Amen.

PAUL VI

PRAYER TO THE VIRGIN
OF GUADALUPE

O Immaculate Virgin,
  Mother of the true God
and Mother of the Church,
from this spot you have manifested
your clemency and your compassion
for all who have recourse to your protection.
Hear the prayer we address to you
with filial confidence,
and present it to your Son Jesus,
our only Redeemer.

Mother of Mercy,
Teacher of hidden and silent sacrifice,
on this day
we sinners consecrate to you,
who come to meet us,
all our being
and all our love.

We also consecrate to you
our life,
our work,
our joys,
our infirmities,
and our sorrows.

Grant to our peoples
peace, justice, and prosperity
so that we may entrust to your care,

our Lady and our Mother,
all that we have
and all that we are.

We wish to be completely yours
and to follow together with you the path
of total fidelity to Jesus Christ
in His Church:
hold us ever lovingly by the hand.

O Virgin of Guadalupe,
Mother of the Americas,
we pray to you for all our bishops,
that they may lead the faithful along the paths
of a dedicated Christian life
and of love and service for God and souls.

See how great is the harvest,
and intercede with the Lord
that He will imbue the whole people of God
with a hunger for holiness
and bestow abundant vocations
of priests and religious,
who are strong in their faith
and zealous dispensors of the mysteries of
    God.

Grant to our homes the grace
of loving and respecting life in its beginnings,
with the same love
with which you conceived in your womb
the life of the Son of God.

Blessed Virgin Mary,
Mother of Fair Love,
protect our families
so that they may always be united
and bless the upbringing of our children.

Our hope,
look upon us with pity,
teach us to go continually to Jesus,
and if we fall
help us to rise again and return to Him
through the confession of our faults
and our sins in the Sacrament of Penance,
which gives peace to the soul.

We beg you to grant us a great love
for all the holy Sacraments,
which are, as it were, the signs
that your Son left us on earth.

Thus, Most Holy Mother,
with the peace of God in our consciences,
with our hearts free from evil and hatred,
we will be able to bring to all others
true joy and true peace,
which come to us
from your Son, our Lord Jesus Christ,
Who with the Father and the Holy Spirit,
lives and reigns for ever and ever.
Amen.

JOHN PAUL II

APPENDIX

POPULAR PRAYERS TO MARY

Hail Mary

HAIL Mary,
full of grace,
the Lord is with you.
Blessed are you among women
and blessed is the fruit of your womb,
Jesus.

Holy Mary,
Mother of God,
pray for us sinners,
now and at the hour of our death.

Holy Mary, Help the Helpless

HOLY Mary,
help the helpless,
strengthen the fearful,
comfort the sorrowful,
pray for the people,
plead for the clergy,
intercede for all women consecrated to God;
may all who keep your sacred commemoration
experience the might of your assistance.

Partial Indulgence.

Remember, O Most Gracious Virgin Mary

REMEMBER, O most gracious Virgin Mary,
that never was it known
that anyone who fled to your protection,
implored your help or sought your intercession,
was left unaided.
Inspired with this confidence,
I fly to you, O Virgin of virgins, my Mother;
to you do I come,
before you I stand, sinful and sorrowful.
O Mother of the Word Incarnate,
despise not my petitions,
but in your mercy hear and answer me.

Partial Indulgence

Hail, Holy Queen

HAIL, holy Queen, Mother of mercy;
hail, our life, our sweetness, and our hope.
To you do we cry,
poor banished children of Eve.
To you do we send up our sighs,
mourning and weeping in this valley of tears.
Turn then, most gracious Advocate,
your eyes of mercy toward us.
And after this our exile

show unto us the blessed fruit of your womb,
  Jesus.
O clement, O loving, O sweet Virgin Mary.

Partial Indulgence.

Prayer of Consecration to Mary

O my Queen and Mother,
  I give myself entirely to you.
To show my devotion to you
I consecrate to you this day
my eyes, ears, mouth, heart,
and whole being without reserve.

Therefore, good Mother,
since I am your own,
keep me and guard me
as your property and possession.

The Angel of the Lord

a) During the year (outside of Paschal Season)

℣. The Angel of the Lord declared unto Mary,
℟. And she conceived of the Holy Spirit.
Hail Mary.
℣. Behold the handmaid of the Lord,
℟. Be it done unto me according to your word.
Hail Mary.
℣. And the Word was made flesh,
℟. And dwelt among us.
Hail Mary.

℣. Pray for us, O holy Mother of God,
℟. That we may be made worthy of the promises of Christ.

Let us pray. Pour forth, we beg You, O Lord,
Your grace into our hearts:
that we, to whom the Incarnation of Christ Your
Son
was made known by the message of an Angel,
may by His Passion and Cross
be brought to the glory of His Resurrection.
Through the same Christ our Lord.

Queen of Heaven

b) During Paschal Season

QUEEN of Heaven, rejoice, alleluia:
For He Whom you merited to bear, alle-
luia,
Has risen, as He said, alleluia.
Pray for us to God, alleluia.

℣. Rejoice and be glad, O Virgin Mary, alleluia.
℟. Because the Lord is truly risen, alleluia.

Let us pray. O God, Who by the Resurrection of
Your Son,
our Lord Jesus Christ,
granted joy to the whole world:
grant, we beg You,
that through the intercession of the Virgin Mary,
His Mother,

we may lay hold of the joys of eternal life.
Through the same Christ our Lord.

A partial indulgence is granted to the faithful, who devoutly recite the above prayers according to the formula indicated for the time of the year.

It is a praiseworthy practice to recite these prayers in the early morning, at noon, and in the evening.

Prayer to Mary, Queen of the Home

O Blessed Virgin Mary,
you are the Mother and Queen of every
Christian family.
When you conceived and gave birth to Jesus,
human motherhood reached its greatest
achievement.
From the time of the Annunciation
you were the living chalice
of the Son of God made Man.
You are the Queen of the home.
As a woman of faith,
you inspire all mothers to transmit faith
to their children.

Watch over our families.
Let the children learn free and loving obedience
inspired by your obedience to God.
Let parents learn dedication and selflessness
based on your unselfish attitude.
Let all families honor you
and remain devoted to you

so that they may be held together
by your example and your intercession.

Our Lady of Fatima

O Most holy Virgin Mary,
Queen of the most holy Rosary,
you were pleased to appear to the children of
Fatima
and reveal a glorious message.
We implore you,
inspire in our hearts a fervent love
for the recitation of the Rosary.
By meditating on the mysteries of the redemption
that are recalled therein
may we obtain the graces and virtues
that we ask, through the merits of Jesus Christ,
our Lord and Redeemer.

Our Lady of Lourdes

O Immaculate Virgin Mary,
you are the refuge of sinners,
the health of the sick,
and the comfort of the afflicted.
By your appearances at the Grotto of Lourdes
you made it a privileged sanctuary
where your favors are given to people
streaming to it from the whole world.

Over the years countless sufferers
have obtained the cure of their infirmities—
whether of soul, mind, or body.
Therefore I come with limitless confidence
to implore your motherly intercessions.
Loving Mother,
obtain the grant of my requests.
Let me strive to imitate your virtues on earth
so that I may one day share your glory in
   heaven.

Our Lady of Guadalupe

OUR Lady of Guadalupe,
   mystical rose,
intercede for the Church,
protect the holy Father,
help all who invoke you in their necessities.
Since you are the ever Virgin Mary
and Mother of the true God,
obtain for us from your most holy Son
the grace of a firm faith and a sure hope
amid the bitterness of life,
as well as an ardent love
and the precious gift of final perseverance.

Prayer of Dedication to Mary

VIRGIN full of goodness,
   Mother of mercy,
I entrust to you my body and my soul,
my thoughts and my actions,
my life and my death.

O my Queen,
come to my aid
and deliver me from the snares of the devil.
Obtain for me the grace of loving
my Lord Jesus Christ, your Son,
with a true and perfect love,
and after Him, O Mary,
of loving you with all my heart
and above all things.

Litany of the Blessed Virgin Mary

LORD, have mercy.
Christ have mercy.
Lord, have mercy.
Christ, hear us.
Christ, graciously hear us.
God, the Father of heaven,
  have mercy on us.
God the Son, Redeemer of
  the world,
  have mercy on us.
God, the Holy Spirit,
  have mercy on us.
Holy Trinity, one God,
  have mercy on us.
Holy Mary, *pray for us.**
Holy Mother of God,
Holy Virgin of virgins,
Mother of Christ,
Mother of the Church,
Mother of Divine grace,
Mother most pure,
Mother most chaste,

Mother inviolate,
Mother most undefiled,
Mother most amiable,
Mother most admirable,
Mother of good counsel,
Mother of our Creator,
Mother of our Savior,
Virgin most prudent,
Virgin most venerable,
Virgin most renowned,
Virgin most powerful,
Virgin most merciful,
Virgin most faithful,
Mirror of justice,
Seat of wisdom,
Cause of our joy,
Spiritual vessel,
Vessel of honor,
Singular vessel of devotion,
Mystical rose,
Tower of David,

* *Pray for us* is repeated after each invocation.

Tower of ivory,
House of gold,
Ark of the covenant,
Gate of heaven,
Morning star,
Health of the sick,
Refuge of sinners,
Comforter of the afflicted,
Help of Christians,
Queen of angels,
Queen of patriarchs,
Queen of prophets,
Queen of apostles,
Queen of martyrs,
Queen of confessors,
Queen of virgins,
Queen of all saints,
Queen conceived without original sin,
Queen assumed into heaven,

Queen of the most holy Rosary,
Queen of families,
Queen of peace,

Lamb of God, you take away the sins of the world; *spare us, O Lord!*

Lamb of God, you take away the sins of the world; *graciously hear us, O Lord!*

Lamb of God, you take away the sins of the world; *have mercy on us.*

℣. Pray for us, O holy Mother of God.

℟. *That we may be made worthy of the promises of Christ.*

L ET us pray.
Grant, we beg You, O Lord God,
that we Your servants
may enjoy lasting health of mind and body,
and by the glorious intercession
of the Blessed Mary, ever Virgin,
be delivered from present sorrow
and enter into the joy of eternal happiness.
Through Christ our Lord.

℟. Amen.